Shared Bread

ILLUSTRATIONS BY CHANTAL MULLER VAN DEN BERGHE
TEXT BY BERNARD HUBLER

Distributed in the United Kingdom and Ireland by:
MATTHEW JAMES PUBLISHING Ltd
19 Wellington Close
Chelmsford, Essex CM1 2EE
Tel: 01245 347 710
Fax: 01245 347 713

Distributed in Canada by:
NOVALIS
49 Front St. E, 2nd Floor
Toronto, ON M5E 1B3
Tel: 1-800-387-7164
Fax (416) 363-9409

Translation by Oliver Todd
Created by Jacques Rey

Quotations from the gospels are from John 6: 1-15 and Matthew 14: 13-21

The gospels tell us what Jesus said and did.
But, in those days, there were no journalists,
no photographers, no tape recorders or camcorders.
Above all, the people who wrote the gospels wanted their
friends to discover who Jesus was. They tell us that he will
be with us always to help us to be happy in life.
So it's not just about reading a nice story,
but about trying to get to know Jesus better.
That's what his friends, the disciples, and the crowd
that followed him, were all trying to do.
They wondered whether or not Jesus was the one
who was going to bring real happiness into the world.

"Jesus climbed the mountain with his disciples."

Jesus loved to go off to the mountains.
Sometimes by himself, sometimes with his disciples.
They could talk about what had been going on,
get some fresh air
or just keep quiet and enjoy the calmness.

There's a lot of noise around us.
Sometimes, it's good to switch the television off
and just think quietly to ourselves.

"He saw a big crowd following him."

But things did not turn out as usual on that day.
Jesus had healed the sick
and spoken in such a comforting way
that the crowd had kept on following him.
Jesus came back and was very moved
by the crowd that was following him.

*Has there ever been a day
when you felt that someone needed you?*

"The disciples said: Send them away so they can go and buy something to eat."

Evening began to fall.
They were far away from the town and the shops.

People were hungry
and the disciples were getting worried
about how everyone was going
to be able to eat.
"It's best to send them away," they said.

*When you have been faced with a big problem,
have you ever felt like just closing your eyes?*

"Jesus said to them:
Give them something to eat yourselves."

Jesus knew what he was going to do
so that the disciples would believe in him.
He says to them: "No! Don't send them away.
Give them something to eat yourselves."
But they said, "That's impossible.
You would need too much money.
We've brought nothing with us and now it's too late."

*Did you know that it's just as important
to ask people to help you
as it is to help others?*

"There was a boy there with five loaves and two fish."

"Open your eyes and look around you," Jesus told them.
"There's a boy with five loaves and two fish.
It's not much but it's something."

You too can produce good results from almost nothing!

"Get them to sit down on the grass," Jesus says.

It was a beautiful sunset.
People were waiting patiently,
not knowing what was going to happen.
"Get them to sit down,"
says Jesus to his disciples.
There was a lot of grass in that place.

What about today?
Do you really trust Jesus?

"Jesus took the bread and fish and said a prayer."

Jesus takes the bread, then the fish.
He raises his eyes to heaven and says a prayer.
One day he will do this same action again
during a meal just before his death.

*Whatever you do for others
can be turned into a prayer.*

"He gave the bread and fish to the disciples to share it out."

The people, seated in small groups,
patiently waited with outstretched hands.
The disciples went round
giving everyone a share of bread and fish.
It was like a giant picnic.

*Many people today hold their hands out,
but nobody gives them anything.*

"Everyone ate as much as they wanted."

Not only did everyone have as much as they wanted,
but there was even some left over.
"Collect it up," says Jesus to his disciples,
"So that nothing is wasted."
And they filled as many baskets
as there are months in the year.

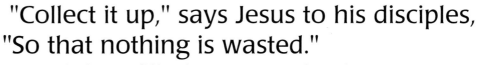

*Let's not waste anything
and let's learn to share,
because many people have nothing at all.*

"The people said: It's him, the one who is to come into the world."

The people were waiting for someone sent by God,
someone who would help them find
a way out of their unhappiness.
What if it was Jesus? Some were not convinced.
Others shook their heads and failed to understand
what had just happened that day before their very eyes.

Like Jesus, can you bring
a bit of happiness to other people today?

In some countries, children are dying of hunger.
In others, food is wasted.
Now the earth can produce enough food
to feed the whole world.
But we need to share more.
Yes, today there are still hungry crowds,
but not just hungry for bread;
they are hungry for justice, love and peace.
Jesus invites us to act like him:
to feed the hungry,
to share our joy and friendship.
But only he can satisfy every hunger.

"Jesus climbed the mountain with his disciples."

6

"He saw a big crowd following him."

8

10

"The disciples said: Send them away so they can go and buy something to eat."

"Jesus said to them: Give them something to eat yourselves."

14

"There was a boy there with five loaves and two fish."

12

"Get them to sit down on the grass," Jesus says.

"Jesus took the bread and fish and said a prayer."

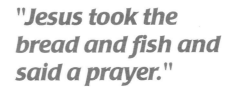

"He gave the bread and fish to the disciples to share it out."

"The people said: It's him, the one who is to come into the world."

"Everyone ate as much as they wanted."

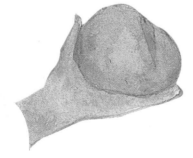

In the same
collection:

Bartimaeus
Zacchaeus
The Good Samaritan
The Paralysed Man
The Calming of the Storm
The Prodigal Son
The Call of the Disciples
The Amazing Catch
The Forgiven Sinner
The Sower
The Disciples from Emmaus